CEREMONIES and RITUALS

MARRIAGE

BY JOANNA BRUNDLE

©2018
Book Life
King's Lynn
Norfolk PE30 4LS

ISBN: 978-1-78637-261-1

All rights reserved
Printed in Malaysia

Written by:
Joanna Brundle

Edited by:
Kirsty Holmes

Designed by:
Daniel Scase

A catalogue record for this book
is available from the British Library.

CONTENTS

Words that look like THIS are explained in the glossary on page 31.

INTRODUCTION

When a couple decide to marry, it is a cause for celebration, whatever their religion or culture. Marriage is celebrated in many different ways around the world. Religious ceremonies and non–religious customs and traditions combine to produce many different kinds of wedding. In this book, we shall be looking at how the world's major religions celebrate marriage. We shall also be looking at some ancient civilisations and at some marriage customs from around the world.

> In Japan, the colour red symbolises life and good fortune. A red umbrella is used to protect the bride and groom from evil spirits.

Have you been to a wedding, or seen one on television? As you read, compare and contrast it with the weddings described.

Couples who want to get married can choose a religious ceremony or a civil ceremony. A civil ceremony has no religious content. Civil ceremonies can take place anywhere that has been licensed to hold weddings, for example a hotel.

In some countries and most religions, marriage is only allowed between a man and a woman. In many countries, and a few religions, people now have equal marriage rights and marriage between couples of any gender is officially recognised.

WEDDING CUSTOMS

During a Chinese wedding ceremony, the couple serve tea to each other's parents to symbolise the introduction of new family members. In some parts of China, brides are expected to cry for an hour a day for 30 days before the wedding. Other female family members join in. Their tears show deep joy and love, rather than sadness!

Wedding tea cups are always red, the colour of good luck in China.

In Fiji, an island in the Pacific Ocean, bridegrooms have to present their future father–in–law with a whale's tooth, before asking for her hand in marriage. In many countries, the bride throws her bouquet over her shoulder at the wedding reception. Whoever catches the bouquet is thought to be next to be married. In Peru, charms attached to ribbons are pulled out of the wedding cake by guests. The lady who pulls out a wedding ring charm will be the next bride.

BROOM JUMPING

In the 1700's, African slaves in America were not officially allowed to marry. Instead, a couple would jump over a broom to symbolise their marriage. Some couples today continue the tradition as a sign of good luck, or simply for fun!

ANCIENT MARRIAGE RITUALS

ANCIENT GREEKS

In ancient Greece, a girl's father would choose a suitable husband for his daughter. Girls had no say in the matter and were usually married at the age of 13. The day before the wedding, the girl made offerings of her childhood toys and clothes to the gods, symbolising the end of her childhood. SACRIFICES such as a lock of hair were made to the goddess Artemis, to ask for her help in making the change from a child to a wife.

Artemis was the Greek goddess of childbirth.

A girl's wedding day began with a bathing RITUAL that was believed to purify her and help her to have children. Her wedding outfit included a VEIL, which was not removed until she had been 'given away' in marriage. After a lavish banquet, the groom grasped his bride's wrist and her father formally handed her over.

The bride was taken by CHARIOT to her new husband's home. Torches were carried by the bride's mother to ward off evil spirits. A specially chosen child handed out bread from a basket during the procession. The bread symbolised the couple's future child and the basket symbolised the cradle. On arrival at her new home, the bride was given fruit, nuts and flowers.

As the father handed over his daughter, he said to the husband 'I give this girl to you for the creation of children.'

The AXLE of the chariot was then burned to symbolise that the bride had a new life as a married woman and could not return to her childhood home.

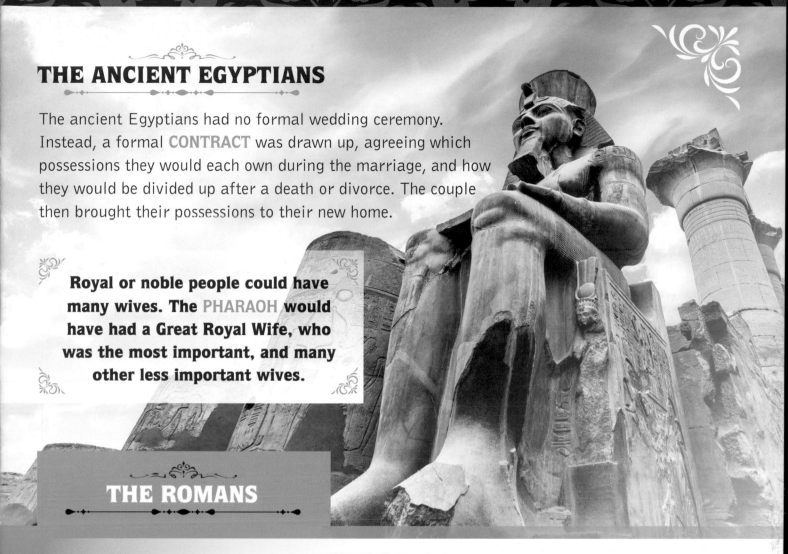

THE ANCIENT EGYPTIANS

The ancient Egyptians had no formal wedding ceremony. Instead, a formal **CONTRACT** was drawn up, agreeing which possessions they would each own during the marriage, and how they would be divided up after a death or divorce. The couple then brought their possessions to their new home.

Royal or noble people could have many wives. The PHARAOH would have had a Great Royal Wife, who was the most important, and many other less important wives.

THE ROMANS

The head of a Roman household, called the paterfamilias, chose marriage partners for his children. He tried to arrange marriages that would increase the wealth or importance of the family.

June was considered to be a lucky month for weddings, which usually took place at the bride's home. Sacrifices were made to the gods and guests enjoyed an elaborate feast. Afterwards, the bride was taken to the groom's home and was lifted over the threshold. This is thought to have been done to honour the goddess, Cardea, who stopped evil spirits from entering the house. In some cultures, it is still customary for the husband to lift his bride over the threshold to their home.

JUDAISM

Followers of Judaism are known as Jews, and family life is of great importance to them. RITES OF PASSAGE, such as a wedding, are joyous celebrations, shared by the whole community.

Jews are strongly encouraged to marry another Jew. Marrying someone from a different religion can be thought of as a rejection of the Jewish faith and IDENTITY.

BEFORE THE WEDDING

THE TORAH

A week before the wedding, a special ceremony called the ufruf is held for the groom at the synagogue, the Jewish temple. He reads from the Jewish holy book, called the Torah, and announces the wedding to the CONGREGATION, who throw sweets at him. Afterwards, refreshments are served in the synagogue.

On the SABBATH before the wedding, the bride's family, female friends and women from the community gather at the bride's home for a celebration. They enjoy cakes and pastries and everyone celebrates with singing and laughter. This is called the Shabbat Kallah. It is traditional for a Jewish bride and groom not to see or speak to one another during the week before the wedding.

THE WEDDING CEREMONY

On the wedding day, the bride and groom **FAST** before the ceremony. This symbolises that they are starting married life in a pure, clean state. A Jewish wedding can take place outside or at the synagogue on any day except the Sabbath. The ceremony must take place under a chuppah – a **CANOPY** held up by four poles. It is usually decorated with flowers.

The chuppah is a symbol of God's protection and of the home the couple will be sharing together.

Before the ceremony, the bride and her attendants wait in a special room in the synagogue. The groom visits her there. In a ritual called the badeken, he places the bride's veil over her face. This symbolises that he intends to clothe and care for her throughout their married life. The veil remains in place until after the ceremony. The bride and groom sign a marriage contract called a ketubah in front of two **WITNESSES**. The ketubah is kept by the bride as proof of the marriage.

The ketubah is often highly decorated and is read out during the ceremony to remind the couple of their responsibilities to each other. Some couples frame the ketubah to display in their home.

After entering the temple together, the bride then walks round the groom seven times. They share a glass of wine together before the groom places a ring on the bride's finger. By accepting the ring, the bride agrees to the marriage. Traditionally, the ring should be a plain band, without any decoration. As he gives the ring to the bride, the groom says 'Behold, you are consecrated to me with this ring, according to the laws of Moses and Israel'. The **RABBI** then recites the Seven Blessings, known as the Sheva Brachot, which praise God and bless the couple.

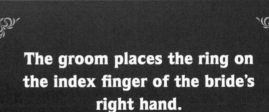

The groom places the ring on the index finger of the bride's right hand.

WEDDING CLOTHES

The bride and groom traditionally wear white to show that their **SOULS** are pure and that their **SINS** have been wiped away. The bride wears a white gown and veil and the groom wears a white robe called a kittel over his suit, or a prayer shawl called a tallit around his shoulders.

The number seven is important in Jewish weddings. It represents God's creation of the world, which Jews believe took six days followed by a seventh day of rest. It symbolises the new life that the couple will create.

AFTER THE CEREMONY

At the end of the ceremony, the groom breaks a wine glass by stamping on it. The glass is wrapped in cloth first, so that there are no injuries!

This ritual symbolises the destruction of the Temple of Solomon in Jerusalem over 2,500 years ago. It reminds Jews of their long history and that there can be sadness even at the happiest times. It also symbolises to the couple that life is fragile and that they must look after one another.

A Jewish bridegroom stamps on a glass wrapped in cloth.

CELEBRATING THE MARRIAGE

Everyone wishes the couple good luck by shouting out 'Mazel tov!' Raisins or sweets may be thrown by the guests as symbols of their good wishes for the couple. The wedding is followed by a celebration banquet that begins with the blessing of a wedding challah – a braided loaf of bread.

Dancing follows the banquet. An energetic dance called the hora is often performed in a circle by the bride and groom and their guests. Everyone surrounds the couple during their first dance as a symbol of support from the community.

The couple break the challah into pieces, giving a piece to each table.

ISLAM

Islam is the second largest religion in the world, after Christianity. Its followers are called Muslims, which means 'obedient ones'. Islam teaches that marriage is the basis of family life and that Muslims should marry and start a family. The marriage of a man and a woman is seen as the joining together of their two families. This joining of families helps to unite the Muslim community. Parents often choose marriage partners for their children.

Although it is becoming uncommon in western cultures, Islam allows a man to have up to four wives at a time. He must treat them all equally and be sure that he can care for all of them and their children. Women are only allowed to have one husband at a time.

THE MARRIAGE CONTRACT

The marriage contract is an agreement between a man and woman that they intend to marry. It is made by agreeing a sum of money called a dowry, known in Islam as the mahr or meher. The mahr belongs to the bride and she may use it as she wishes. It is sometimes given in two parts, some before the wedding and some throughout the bride's life.

The mahr may be presented in an embroidered purse or decorative box.

BEFORE THE WEDDING

About a week before the wedding ceremony, the bride and groom traditionally hold a dholki, a party with singing and dancing. The word 'dholki' means 'drum' and the celebration includes the banging of a drum. The night before the wedding, the mehendi ceremony takes place. The hands and feet of the bride and other female family members are decorated with beautiful patterns, using a dye called henna. The bride usually wears yellow for the mehendi ceremony. The painting of the designs is done by female friends and family members of the bride. Sometimes the groom also attends the mehendi ceremony and receives a henna dot in the palm of his hands.

WEDDING CLOTHES

Many Muslim brides now choose to wear a white wedding gown, often including a white **HIJAB**. Traditionally, Muslim brides wear a red ghagra; a full length, pleated skirt with a long blouse, embroidered with gold thread. Muslim men either wear a western–style suit or a traditional sherwani, a long coat with sleeves and a high collar, worn with a **TURBAN**.

This Muslim bride is wearing a traditional red and gold gown.

THE NIKAH CEREMONY

The marriage contract is signed in a ceremony called the nikah. The bride's father offers his daughter in marriage at the previously agreed dowry amount. Sometimes the groom proposes to the bride, by giving the details of the mahr. The bride and groom show that they are both free to make their own decision by saying three times 'qabal', which means 'I accept'. Everyone calls upon Allah as a witness to the agreement.

Allah is the Muslim name for God.

The ceremony is always attended by the fathers of the bride and groom, known as walises, and by at least two adult male witnesses. Witnesses sign the contract along with the bride and groom, making the marriage legal.

It is customary for the women and men attending the ceremony, including the bride and groom, to sit separately.

After the contract has been signed, the couple traditionally share sweet dates, to remind them of the sweetness of the Qur'an, the Islamic holy book.

THIS MUSLIM MARRIAGE CEREMONY IS TAKING PLACE AT THE MOSQUE.

The nikah ceremony often includes prayers and verses from the Qur'an. It may be held at the mosque, the Muslim place of worship, but it often takes place at a family home. No special religious official has to attend the ceremony but an **IMAM** will sometimes give a **SERMON**. Some mosques have marriage officers called ma'zouns, who oversee the ceremony.

THE WALIMAH

The prophet Muhammad said that a marriage should be announced publicly with the beating of drums. Therefore, Muslims traditionally hold a large celebration, called the walimah, after the nikah ceremony. They invite family, friends and members of the Muslim community to join them in feasting and in celebrating their marriage. It is said that a whole goat was cooked and offered to guests at one of Muhammad's walimahs, so some couples follow his example and serve a whole goat or sheep.

The feast may include a special wedding cake.

The walimah is traditionally hosted by the bridegroom's family. Men and women may be seated separately. The bride and groom sometimes sit on decorated seats, rather like thrones, raised up on a platform. This is so that they can be seen clearly by all the guests, who offer gifts and money. The bride's father gives her hand to the groom and asks him to protect her. The couple then leave for the husband's house. The guests may throw rice, sweets and dried fruit as the couple leave.

Sugared almonds are traditionally offered to guests at the walimah.

The bride is welcomed by her new mother–in–law, who holds a copy of the Qur'an over her head as she enters her new home.

CHRISTIANITY

Christianity is the largest religion in the world, with followers, called Christians, in many parts of the world. The Christian holy book, the Bible, teaches Christians to love one another. It emphasises the importance of marriage to confirm the love between a man and a woman. Christians look upon marriage as a gift from God, which involves lifelong COMMITMENT.

Marriage is also known as Holy Matrimony.

BEFORE THE WEDDING

Christians usually choose their own marriage partner. Traditionally, the bridegroom asks the bride's father for her hand in marriage. During the groom's proposal of marriage to his bride, he may present her with a ring, often set with a diamond or other gemstone. She wears the ring on the fourth finger of her left hand, as a sign of the engagement. In some branches of the Christian Church, a wedding is publicly announced in church by the reading of the banns.

The banns are a public announcement of a wedding and are read during three Sunday church services before the wedding.

A Christian marriage ceremony takes place in church and is conducted by a priest. Traditionally, the bride wears a white gown, to symbolise her purity.

In many cultures, it is considered unlucky for the groom to see the bride's dress before the wedding.

The bride is usually attended by bridesmaids, who provide assistance during and after the ceremony. The bridegroom is supported by a best man, sometimes known as a groomsman. The best man is responsible for looking after the wedding rings that the bride and groom exchange during the ceremony.

Wedding rings are a sign of marriage. The unbroken, circular shape symbolises the never—ending love of the couple and of Jesus' love for his Church.

The bride usually walks up the aisle with her father and is met by the groom. The priest explains the purpose of marriage and the bride's father hands the bride over to the groom. The couple make solemn promises to one another to be faithful, and to care for one another throughout their lives. These promises are called their vows. The rings are blessed and exchanged and the priest then announces that the couple are husband and wife. This is called the proclamation. The bride and groom kiss one another and the congregation may applaud.

The priest uses his **STOLE** to wrap together the hands of the bride and groom. He asks that nobody should divide they who have been joined together by God.

During the ceremony, hymns are sung and passages from the Bible are read, often by a family member. The priest gives a sermon, usually offering the couple guidance for their new life together. Prayers are said for the couple and, at the end of the ceremony, the priest asks God to bless them in their married life. In order to make the marriage legal, the bride and groom and two witnesses sign a **MARRIAGE REGISTER**. The couple are given a marriage certificate as legal proof of the marriage.

CONFETTI

As the couple leave church it is tradition that their family and friends throw confetti over them. This symbolises the good wishes of the guests for health, good luck and children for the couple.

> **Nowadays, confetti is usually made of tissue paper or dried flower petals but people used to throw grains of rice, symbolising FERTILITY.**

Church bells have been rung at Christian wedding ceremonies since **MEDIEVAL** times. People believed that bell–ringing warded off evil spirits. Bells were also used to let the whole community know that a wedding had taken place. It is a tradition that has become popular all around the world as a sign of celebration and joy, marking the start of the couple's married life.

THE WEDDING BREAKFAST

After the ceremony, a reception is held,
traditionally hosted by the bride's parents.
The couple and their guests enjoy a meal,
known as the wedding breakfast. After the
meal, the couple cut the wedding cake,
traditionally both holding the knife,
to symbolise their joining together.
Music and dancing follow.

**The wedding cake was a tradition begun by the Romans. They ate the cake
during the marriage ceremony, rather than waiting until the feast afterwards!**

THE BIBLE

The Bible contains letters written by some of Jesus' disciples, or followers. Paul's letter to the Corinthians speaks of what Christian love means. It is often read at weddings, to offer guidance to the couple. It reminds Christians of the importance of love for one another. It teaches that love means being kind and patient, never boastful or angry, and that, without love, nothing else is important.

**The Bible says that Jesus
performed his first miracle
at a wedding at Cana,
turning water into wine.**

In Church, the Bible is placed on a stand called
a lectern. Passages from the Bible are read at
all church services, including weddings.

HINDUISM

Hinduism is the world's oldest religion. Followers of Hinduism, called Hindus, believe that marriage is one of 16 important events in a person's life. These rites of passage are celebrated with ceremonies called samskars.

The marriage samskar is called Vivaha.

Hindus value marriage highly and believe that getting married is their sacred duty to God. Hindu wedding rituals vary from place to place, but there are some important elements that are the same everywhere.

BEFORE THE WEDDING

Garlands

Hindu couples have a formal engagement ceremony called a misri, attended by both families. The couple exchange garlands as a sign of welcoming each other, and rings to symbolise a long, happy marriage.

THE MEHNDI CEREMONY

During the afternoon before the wedding, Hindu brides celebrate the mehndi ceremony. Their hands and feet are painted with beautiful designs, using henna dye. This process takes several hours to complete!

The night before the wedding, the bride and groom each celebrate a religious ceremony, called Ghari puja, separately with their families. They make offerings of rice, wheat grains, coconut and a yellow spice called turmeric to the gods and ask for blessings on the marriage.

Hindus use coconut as a symbol of fertility and of God's presence.

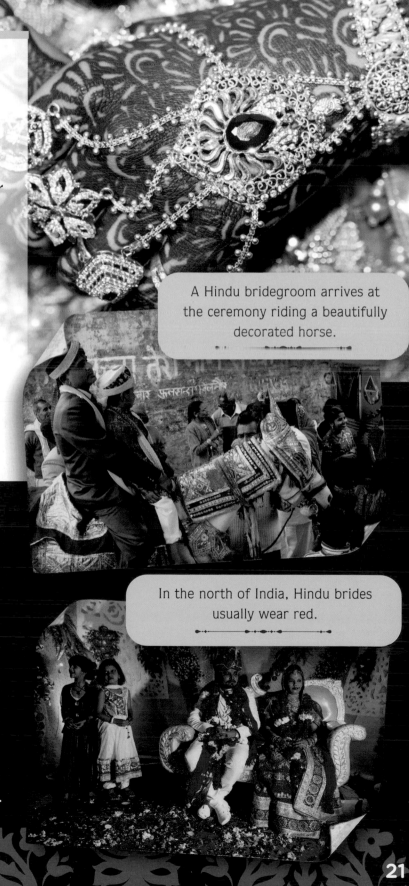

PREPARING THE BRIDE

Before she puts on her wedding outfit, a Hindu bride goes through a cleansing ritual, using turmeric and scented oils. Brides wear a silk **SARI** and a veil or scarf. Everything is beautifully decorated with embroidery in silver and gold thread and with jewels and pearls. The colour of the sari varies in different regions. Brides from southern India, for example, traditionally wear a yellow sari with a gold belt. Hindu brides wear a great deal of silver or gold jewellery, including necklaces, bracelets, earrings and rings. They often wear decorative makeup and add flowers and jewels in their hair.

A Hindu bridegroom arrives at the ceremony riding a beautifully decorated horse.

THE BRIDEGROOM

The bridegroom wears loose trousers, called dhoti, and a satin shirt. On his head he wears a wedding turban called a safa, decorated with pearls and feathers. The bridegroom travels to the ceremony in a noisy procession, with singing and dancing, called the vara yatra. He may arrive on horseback, or even riding an elephant! He is met by the bride's mother. Using a red powder called kumkum, she places a **TILAK** mark on his forehead as a sign of good luck.

In the north of India, Hindu brides usually wear red.

THE MARRIAGE CEREMONY

The marriage ceremony takes place under a wedding canopy, called a mandap. The mandap is supported by four posts, representing the four parents of the bride and groom. The bride is brought to the mandap by one of her uncles. In order to purify the bride and groom for their new life together, the bride's parents wash the couple's feet with milk and water. They then place garlands around their necks. Their daughter's right hand is placed in the groom's right hand, to symbolise the gift of the daughter to the groom's family. This ritual is called hasta–melap. The bride's sari is then tied to the bridegroom's scarf and the couple's right hands are loosely tied together with sacred thread.

FIRE

The priest lights a ritual fire, known as an agni, to represent Vishnu, the supreme Hindu god. The bride and groom walk round the fire four times, praying and exchanging promises of duty, love, faithfulness and respect. Family members throw rice, **GHEE** and flowers into the fire and ask for the gods' blessings on the couple.

Hindus believe that walking round the fire four times symbolises the four stages of life, called ashramas.

A mangala sutra necklace is worn by a Hindu woman to show she is married. It is often given to the bride by her mother–in–law on her wedding day.

THE SAPTAPADI RITUAL

The saptapadi ritual takes place at the end of the marriage ceremony and is the most important part of the wedding. The couple take seven steps together while chanting seven vows. The steps symbolise food, support for one another, wealth, happiness, children, togetherness throughout life and loyal friendship. When the saptapadi ritual is complete, the couple are legally married.

The saptapadi vows are traditionally spoken in Sanskrit, a very old Indian language.

The bride is welcomed into the groom's family home with blessings from her new husband's parents. She sprinkles milk around her new home to show respect. A ceremony called datar then takes place. The bride gives her husband some salt, which he returns to her. They do this three times and she then repeats the process with family members. It symbolises that she will mix in happily with her new family and will add to family life.

AFTER THE MARRIAGE CEREMONY

A reception for all the guests follows the ceremony. Hindu families often go to great expense to provide a lavish celebration, which may go on for several days. Hundreds of guests may be invited. Wealthy Hindu families in India often invite the whole village.

When the bride eventually leaves her family home, she throws rice and coins over her shoulder to thank her parents.

The newly-married couple traditionally look towards the polestar, which always appears to remain fixed in the night sky. This ritual symbolises that their marriage will last.

SIKHISM

Sikhism was founded in India in the 1400s by a man called Guru Nanak. Guru means 'teacher'.

Followers of Sikhism are called Sikhs. A Sikh wedding, called anand karaj, meaning 'ceremony of bliss', is always a joyful celebration. Sikhs are encouraged to marry another Sikh and family opinion on the choice of a partner is important. But Guru Nanak taught that all people are equal in God's eyes and both the bride and groom have to agree to the marriage. Marriage is seen as a joining together of two families. Before the wedding, the families get to know one another and may visit each other and enjoy meals together.

THE ENGAGEMENT

When everyone agrees that the couple should marry, a formal ceremony called the thaka takes place, in which the couple promise to marry one another. The future bride's father blesses his future son-in-law by making a tilak mark on his forehead with saffron paste. To mark the kurmai, or engagement, the bride is given a ring. Sometimes, she also gives her future husband a gold ring.

Saffron is a bright orangey-yellow dye, made from dried parts of the crocus flower.

THE MARRIAGE CEREMONY

A Sikh marriage ceremony normally takes place in the morning, usually at the bride's local temple. The bridegroom arrives in a noisy procession called the baraat, with singing and dancing.

The groom is met by the bride's female family members, who sprinkle him with rose water. He is then greeted by the bride's male family members, in order from the oldest to the youngest. Flower garlands are exchanged, and gifts of money and clothing are made to the groom, to symbolise the joining of the families. The families eat a meal, called the milni, together.

Sikh weddings begin with the Asa Di Var, a hymn that is sung each morning at the Gurdwara, the Sikh place of worship. The ardas, a prayer that Sikhs always say before important tasks, is read out. The person conducting the ceremony explains the Sikh ideal that marriage is the joining together of two bodies in one soul.

The couple bow to the Guru Granth Sahib, the Sikh holy book, as a sign of respect. Sikhs believe that it must be shown the same respect that would be given to a human Guru.

Sikh weddings are often conducted by a Sikh priest, called a Granthi, but any wise, respected Sikh man or woman can be chosen by the families.

Sikhs often mark important events like marriages by holding an akhand paath, a non-stop reading of the Guru Granth Sahib. It takes 48 hours and is usually timed to be completed at dawn on the day of the special occasion.

The bride's father then places the end of the groom's scarf, known as a palla, in his daughter's hand. These actions symbolise the spiritual joining together of the couple and that the bride is leaving her father's protection, to join her husband.

THE LAVAAN

Four verses of the wedding hymn, called the Lavaan, are sung or read out loud. The first two verses remind the couple that they must live as God would wish them to and that they must be selfless and loving to one another. The next two verses speak of their love of God and remind them that in marriage, human love blends with the love of God.

At some Gurdwaras professional singers and musicians, called ragis, perform the Laavan.

At the end of each verse, the couple bow to the Guru Granth Sahib and the groom leads his bride around it in a clockwise direction. They hold on to the bridegroom's scarf throughout. Walking round the Guru Granth Sahib symbolises that the couple accept the importance of its teachings and that it is central to their lives.

A Sikh bridegroom leads his bride around the Guru Granth Sahib.

26

AFTER THE CEREMONY

The ceremony ends with the guests sharing a sweet dish called karah parshad.

After every service at the Gurdwara, including weddings, the congregation share a meal together, called the langar. The place in the Gurdwara where it is eaten is also called the langar. The groom's parents may also host a lavish lunch for many more guests, with food, drinks, bhangra music and dancing.

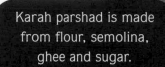

Karah parshad is made from flour, semolina, ghee and sugar.

The Guru Granth Sahib is kept covered when it is not being read. A Sikh bridegroom sometimes marks his marriage by presenting a new silk covering, called a rumala.

Bhangra Dancing

Can you spot the groom's kirpan and the bride's kaleere?

SIKH WEDDING WEAR

Sikh brides in India traditionally wear a red **SALWAR KAMEEZ**, decorated with embroidery and beading. Red symbolises prosperity and good luck. Brides may wear other colours, especially in other countries. The head and shoulders are covered with a shawl called a dupatta. Sikh brides wear a great deal of jewellery, including a heavy gold necklace called a rani haar and traditional red and white bangles. Gold or silver ornaments called kaleere are attached to the bangles and hang from the wrists. A Sikh bridegroom wears a coloured turban, as a sign of respect to God. He carries a kirpan, a short sword, to symbolise his new role as protector of his wife.

27

BUDDHISM

Buddhism began in India, around 2,500 years ago. It is based on the teachings of a man named Siddhartha Gautama. He became known as the Buddha, meaning 'enlightened one', because of his wisdom and understanding of the world. Buddhists believe that marriage is not a religious duty. Everyone should be free to choose whether they get married and whether they have children. A Buddhist marriage involves commitment from the bride and groom that they will live according to the teachings of the Buddha. Faithfulness, loyalty, respect and treating one another as equals are very important.

MARRIAGE CLOTHES

The families of the future bride and groom meet to compare and match their **HOROSCOPES**. A suitable day for the engagement is chosen. The formal engagement is known as Nanchang. Gifts of meat and rice are made to the woman's mother and the man traditionally presents his new fiancée with a gift. The couple usually live together at the home of either set of parents after the engagement.

The gift to the fiancée may be a piece of jewellery, such as this ring, or a piece of land.

THE MARRIAGE

There are no formal teachings about the marriage ceremony in the Buddhist faith. Buddhists celebrate marriage in different ways, according to the customs of the country where they live. Buddhist weddings often take the form of a civil ceremony, followed by a blessing in a Buddhist temple. The civil ceremony ensures that the couple are married according to the law.

An **ASTROLOGER** studies the horoscopes of the couple and the date of the wedding is fixed, based on their advice.

MARRIAGE CLOTHES

The colour of the outfits worn by the bride and groom are traditionally decided according to their horoscopes. Red and gold are often chosen and black is considered unlucky. In western countries, white is becoming a popular choice for the bride. The traditional outfit for a Buddhist bride is a full length gown, known as a Bhaku, made of a special type of material called brocade. A silk blouse with sleeves, calleda Hanju, is worn over the top.

Brocade is a rich, silk fabric, woven with a raised pattern, usually with gold or silver thread.

This traditional red and gold brocade dress is worn with a decorative belt.

The bridegroom also wears a Bhaku, made of brocade. It has long sleeves, is full length and is worn with a waistcoat called a Lajha. He also wears a brocade cap and sash. Modern Buddhist bridegrooms may wear a western style suit.

MARRIAGE CEREMONIES

Buddhist blessing and commitment ceremonies in the temple begin with the bride and groom bowing in front of an image of the Buddha. They then light candles and incense and place flowers at a SHRINE to the Buddha.

Candles are lit and flowers are placed at the Buddha's shrine before the ceremony begins.

The couple may recite traditional wedding vows, promising love, kindness and consideration. Buddhist monks may chant special verses, including the Pancasila, or Five Precepts, which give Buddhists guidance about how to live their lives.

The parents of the couple then place a loop of white string over the heads of the bride and groom, symbolising that they are joined together. Sometimes, the thread is passed around all the guests, to show that they are all part of the Buddhist community. After the ceremony, it is traditional for the couple to make gifts of food or money to the monks at the temple. The guests then enjoy a wedding feast with music and dancing.

These Buddhist monks are holding the white thread at a wedding ceremony.

Buddhist monks may bless the couple by ANOINTING their foreheads with three dots of white paste that has been blessed during the ceremony.

GLOSSARY

axle	the bar on which a wheel or wheels turn
anointing	smearing or rubbing with oil or paste as part of a religious ceremony
astrologer	a person who studies the positions and movements of the planets
canopy	a cloth or covering held up over something
chariot	a two-wheeled vehicle, pulled by a horse
commitment	a promise or pledge to do something
congregation	a group of people who have come together for worship
contract	a legal agreement
fast	to not eat or drink, usually for religious reasons
fertility	the ability to have children
ghee	clarified butter
hijab	a head covering worn in public by some Muslim women
horoscopes	predictions about a person's future, based on the position of the planets at the time of their birth
identity	a person's view of who they are
imam	a religious teacher in the Islamic faith
marriage register	an official list or record of weddings that have taken place
medieval	relating to the period in history from about 1100 to 1453 AD
Pharaoh	a ruler in ancient Egypt
rabbi	a teacher of Judaism
rites of passage	important events, particularly religious events, in a person's life
ritual	ordered actions that take place during religious ceremonies
Sabbath	the Jewish day of rest, beginning at nightfall on Friday and ending at nightfall on Saturday
sacrifices	offerings of possessions to the gods
salwar kameez	an outfit comprising of a pair of light, loose trousers, fitted round the ankles, worn with a long tunic
sari	a piece of clothing made from a single length of cloth, draped around the body
sermon	a talk on a religious matter, given during a church service
shrine	a holy place or a place of worship that is marked by a building or some other construction
sins	bad acts that are seen to be against a god's will
souls	the spiritual, rather than physical part of a person, that is considered to live forever
stole	a scarf, usually made of silk, worn by a priest
tilak	a mark worn on the forehead
turban	a man's headdress, made of a length of fabric wrapped around the head, worn especially by Muslims and Sikhs
veil	a piece of fine material, worn by a woman to hide her face
witnesses	people who are present at the signing of an important document, who then sign the document themselves

INDEX

PHOTO CREDITS

Front Cover – India Picture. 2 – Kyryk Ivan. 4 – Pakpoom Phummee, Kim Ruoff. 5 – a.for.amazing, oliveromg, In The Light Photography. 6 – Gilmanshin. 7 – Graficam Ahmed Saeed, Bukhta Yurii. 8 – ungvar. 9 – Suprun Vitaly, Ekaterina Lin. 10 – david156, york777, IVASHstudio. 11 – TI, Joshua Rainey Photography. 12 – SHAH AIZAD. 13 – Olena Zaskochenko, Kdonmuang. 14 – Hamizan Yusof, Ninell, ZouZou. 15 – Fathulkamar Mohd Sharif, Chudovska. 16 – MNStudio. 17 – Sergiy Zavgorodny, MNStudio. 18 – Joe Gough, Wedding Stock Photo, Kynamuia. 19 – KMW Photography, Jacek Wojnarowski. 20 – Mukesh Kumar, NikD90, NIKS ADS. 21 – tahirsphotography, De Visu, StanislavBeloglazov. 22 – Sankalp Vishwakarma, espies, Nadina. 23 – Milind Arvind Ketkar. 24 – patrimonio designs ltd, India Picture. 25 – Thanakrit Sathavornmanee, Tyshchenko Photography. 26 – Tyshchenko Photography. 27 – Muhammad Shairazi, Tyshchenko Photography. 28 – Patryk Kosmider, Tharin Sinlapachai, 29 – Pavel L Photo and Video, I AM NIKOM. 30 – wandee007, vasanty, bireleycrayon, Karn Samanvorawong, Gina Smith. Border on all pages: PremiumVector.